MY HOMESCHOOL
PLANNER

BY
_____

Inspire My Homeschool Planner 2025: Bringing clarity, order and structure into your learning schedule.
By Michelle Morrow and Sarah Graham © 2024
ISBN: 978-1-7636291-2-7

All rights reserved. No part of this publication may be reproduced, stored in a retrieval system, or transmitted in any other form or means – electronic, mechanical, photocopying, recording or otherwise, without the prior permission of the copyright owner and the publisher or as provided by Australian law.
All enquiries to:
My Homeschool PTY LTD,
NSW, Australia
https://myhomeschool.com

HOMESCHOOL PLANNING

Keeping a simple homeschool planner gives focus to your routines and goals. It also aids record keeping and helps your day run smoothly.

This homeschool planner is a tool to help you homeschool. We've included:

- Yearly Calendar for 2024, 2025 & 2026
- Quarterly Planning Reviews
- A Week at a Glance
- A Month at a Glance
- List Pages for:
  - Art, Music and Poetry Appreciation: Keep a record of composers, artists and poets you study as a family. This is an ongoing list and will be updated as the year goes on.
  - Movies & Documentaries: Write down what they are watching so you have a record for the future.
  - Field Trips & Nature Walks: This form will remind you to plan field trips and remember where you went.
  - Homeschool Expenses: Make a wish list of items you want to buy for your homeschool.
  - Book Lists: Use for read alouds completed, library books your child reads and books you want to read or purchase.
  - Books on Loan: If you lend a friend a book, this will remind you who you lent it to.
- Student Notes: This is for specific notes related to planning for a specific child's studies. You might like to add assignment due dates or skills achieved.
- Project Pages: Use this to record projects that you might want to achieve as a family. Include things like making an item of clothing, redecorating a room, planting a vegetable garden or making a shelf. You may also like to add your own projects.
- General Notes

Happy Homeschooling!

2024 Calendar

January
S	M	T	W	T	F	S
	1	2	3	4	5	6
7	8	9	10	11	12	13
14	15	16	17	18	19	20
21	22	23	24	25	26	27
28	29	30	31			

February
S	M	T	W	T	F	S
				1	2	3
4	5	6	7	8	9	10
11	12	13	14	15	16	17
18	19	20	21	22	23	24
25	26	27	28	29		

March
S	M	T	W	T	F	S
					1	2
3	4	5	6	7	8	9
10	11	12	13	14	15	16
17	18	19	20	21	22	23
24	25	26	27	28	29	30
31						

April
S	M	T	W	T	F	S
	1	2	3	4	5	6
7	8	9	10	11	12	13
14	15	16	17	18	19	20
21	22	23	24	25	26	27
28	29	30				

May
S	M	T	W	T	F	S
			1	2	3	4
5	6	7	8	9	10	11
12	13	14	15	16	17	18
19	20	21	22	23	24	25
26	27	28	29	30	31	

June
S	M	T	W	T	F	S
						1
2	3	4	5	6	7	8
9	10	11	12	13	14	15
16	17	18	19	20	21	22
23	24	25	26	27	28	29
30						

July
S	M	T	W	T	F	S
	1	2	3	4	5	6
7	8	9	10	11	12	13
14	15	16	17	18	19	20
21	22	23	24	25	26	27
28	29	30	31			

August
S	M	T	W	T	F	S
				1	2	3
4	5	6	7	8	9	10
11	12	13	14	15	16	17
18	19	20	21	22	23	24
25	26	27	28	29	30	31

September
S	M	T	W	T	F	S
1	2	3	4	5	6	7
8	9	10	11	12	13	14
15	16	17	18	19	20	21
22	23	24	25	26	27	28
29	30					

October
S	M	T	W	T	F	S
		1	2	3	4	5
6	7	8	9	10	11	12
13	14	15	16	17	18	19
20	21	22	23	24	25	26
27	28	29	30	31		

November
S	M	T	W	T	F	S
					1	2
3	4	5	6	7	8	9
10	11	12	13	14	15	16
17	18	19	20	21	22	23
24	25	26	27	28	29	30

December
S	M	T	W	T	F	S
1	2	3	4	5	6	7
8	9	10	11	12	13	14
15	16	17	18	19	20	21
22	23	24	25	26	27	28
29	30	31				

Notes

 # 2025 Calendar

January

S	M	T	W	T	F	S
			1	2	3	4
5	6	7	8	9	10	11
12	13	14	15	16	17	18
19	20	21	22	23	24	25
26	27	28	29	30	31	

February

S	M	T	W	T	F	S
						1
2	3	4	5	6	7	8
9	10	11	12	13	14	15
16	17	18	19	20	21	22
23	24	25	26	27	28	

March

S	M	T	W	T	F	S
						1
2	3	4	5	6	7	8
9	10	11	12	13	14	15
16	17	18	19	20	21	22
23	24	25	26	27	28	29
30	31					

April

S	M	T	W	T	F	S
		1	2	3	4	5
6	7	8	9	10	11	12
13	14	15	16	17	18	19
20	21	22	23	24	25	26
27	28	29	30			

May

S	M	T	W	T	F	S
				1	2	3
4	5	6	7	8	9	10
11	12	13	14	15	16	17
18	19	20	21	22	23	24
25	26	27	28	29	30	31

June

S	M	T	W	T	F	S
1	2	3	4	5	6	7
8	9	10	11	12	13	14
15	16	17	18	19	20	21
22	23	24	25	26	27	28
29	30					

July

S	M	T	W	T	F	S
		1	2	3	4	5
6	7	8	9	10	11	12
13	14	15	16	17	18	19
20	21	22	23	24	25	26
27	28	29	30	31		

August

S	M	T	W	T	F	S
					1	2
3	4	5	6	7	8	9
10	11	12	13	14	15	16
17	18	19	20	21	22	23
24	25	26	27	28	29	30
31						

September

S	M	T	W	T	F	S
	1	2	3	4	5	6
7	8	9	10	11	12	13
14	15	16	17	18	19	20
21	22	23	24	25	26	27
28	29	30				

October

S	M	T	W	T	F	S
			1	2	3	4
5	6	7	8	9	10	11
12	13	14	15	16	17	18
19	20	21	22	23	24	25
26	27	28	29	30	31	

November

S	M	T	W	T	F	S
						1
2	3	4	5	6	7	8
9	10	11	12	13	14	15
16	17	18	19	20	21	22
23	24	25	26	27	28	29
30						

December

S	M	T	W	T	F	S
	1	2	3	4	5	6
7	8	9	10	11	12	13
14	15	16	17	18	19	20
21	22	23	24	25	26	27
28	29	30	31			

Notes

 # 2026 Calendar

January

S	M	T	W	T	F	S
				1	2	3
4	5	6	7	8	9	10
11	12	13	14	15	16	17
18	19	20	21	22	23	24
25	26	27	28	29	30	31

February

S	M	T	W	T	F	S
1	2	3	4	5	6	7
8	9	10	11	12	13	14
15	16	17	18	19	20	21
22	23	24	25	26	27	28

March

S	M	T	W	T	F	S
1	2	3	4	5	6	7
8	9	10	11	12	13	14
15	16	17	18	19	20	21
22	23	24	25	26	27	28
29	30	31				

April

S	M	T	W	T	F	S
			1	2	3	4
5	6	7	8	9	10	11
12	13	14	15	16	17	18
19	20	21	22	23	24	25
26	27	28	29	30		

May

S	M	T	W	T	F	S
					1	2
3	4	5	6	7	8	9
10	11	12	13	14	15	16
17	18	19	20	21	22	23
24	25	26	27	28	29	30
31						

June

S	M	T	W	T	F	S
	1	2	3	4	5	6
7	8	9	10	11	12	13
14	15	16	17	18	19	20
21	22	23	24	25	26	27
28	29	30				

July

S	M	T	W	T	F	S
			1	2	3	4
5	6	7	8	9	10	11
12	13	14	15	16	17	18
19	20	21	22	23	24	25
26	27	28	29	30	31	

August

S	M	T	W	T	F	S
						1
2	3	4	5	6	7	8
9	10	11	12	13	14	15
16	17	18	19	20	21	22
23	24	25	26	27	28	29
30	31					

September

S	M	T	W	T	F	S
		1	2	3	4	5
6	7	8	9	10	11	12
13	14	15	16	17	18	19
20	21	22	23	24	25	26
27	28	29	30			

October

S	M	T	W	T	F	S
				1	2	3
4	5	6	7	8	9	10
11	12	13	14	15	16	17
18	19	20	21	22	23	24
25	26	27	28	29	30	31

November

S	M	T	W	T	F	S
1	2	3	4	5	6	7
8	9	10	11	12	13	14
15	16	17	18	19	20	21
22	23	24	25	26	27	28
29	30					

December

S	M	T	W	T	F	S
		1	2	3	4	5
6	7	8	9	10	11	12
13	14	15	16	17	18	19
20	21	22	23	24	25	26
27	28	29	30	31		

Notes

2025

Quarterly 1 Notes

QUARTERLY PLANNER (DATES)

_____
_____
_____
_____
_____
_____
_____
_____
_____
_____
_____
_____
_____
_____
_____

NOTES

_____
_____
_____
_____
_____
_____
_____
_____
_____
_____
_____
_____
_____
_____
_____

STUDENT HELP AT A GLANCE

MONDAY	
TUESDAY	
WEDNESDAY	
THURSDAY	
FRIDAY	
SATURDAY	
SUNDAY	

BOOKS TO GET

_____
_____
_____
_____
_____
_____

PEOPLE TO CONTACT

_____
_____
_____
_____
_____
_____

JANUARY

MONDAY	TUESDAY	WEDNESDAY	THURSDAY
30	31	1	2
6	7	8	9
13	14	15	16
20	21	22	23
27	28	29	30

FRIDAY	SATURDAY	SUNDAY
3	4	5
10	11	12
17	18	19
24	25	26
31	1	2

notes

MY WEEK

DECEMBER - JANUARY

30 MONDAY	31 TUESDAY	1 WEDNESDAY
2 THURSDAY	3 FRIDAY	4 SATURDAY
5 SUNDAY	NOTES	

MY WEEK

JANUARY

6 MONDAY	**7** TUESDAY	**8** WEDNESDAY
9 THURSDAY	**10** FRIDAY	**11** SATURDAY
12 SUNDAY	NOTES	

MY WEEK

JANUARY

13 MONDAY	14 TUESDAY	15 WEDNESDAY
16 THURSDAY	17 FRIDAY	18 SATURDAY
19 SUNDAY	NOTES	

MY WEEK  JANUARY

20 MONDAY	21 TUESDAY	22 WEDNESDAY
23 THURSDAY	24 FRIDAY	25 SATURDAY
26 SUNDAY	NOTES	

FEBRUARY

MONDAY	TUESDAY	WEDNESDAY	THURSDAY
27	28	29	30
3	4	5	6
10	11	12	13
17	18	19	20
24	25	26	27

FRIDAY	SATURDAY	SUNDAY
31	1	2
7	8	9
14	15	16
21	22	23
28	1	2

notes

MY WEEK

JANUARY - FEBRUARY

27 MONDAY	28 TUESDAY	29 WEDNESDAY

30 THURSDAY	31 FRIDAY	1 SATURDAY

2 SUNDAY	NOTES

MY WEEK

FEBRUARY

| 3 MONDAY | 4 TUESDAY | 5 WEDNESDAY |

| 6 THURSDAY | 7 FRIDAY | 8 SATURDAY |

| 9 SUNDAY | NOTES |

MY WEEK

FEBRUARY

| 10 MONDAY | 11 TUESDAY | 12 WEDNESDAY |

| 13 THURSDAY | 14 FRIDAY | 15 SATURDAY |

| 16 SUNDAY | NOTES |

MY WEEK

FEBRUARY

17 MONDAY	18 TUESDAY	19 WEDNESDAY
20 THURSDAY	21 FRIDAY	22 SATURDAY

23 SUNDAY	NOTES

MARCH

MONDAY	TUESDAY	WEDNESDAY	THURSDAY
24	25	26	27
3	4	5	6
10	11	12	13
17	18	19	20
24	25	26	27
31	1	2	3

FRIDAY	SATURDAY	SUNDAY	notes
28	1	2	
7	8	9	
14	15	16	
21	22	23	
28	29	30	
4	5	6	

MY WEEK  FEBRUARY - MARCH

24 MONDAY	25 TUESDAY	26 WEDNESDAY
27 THURSDAY	28 FRIDAY	1 SATURDAY
2 SUNDAY	NOTES	

MY WEEK

MARCH

3 MONDAY	4 TUESDAY	5 WEDNESDAY
6 THURSDAY	7 FRIDAY	8 SATURDAY
9 SUNDAY	NOTES	

MY WEEK  MARCH

10 MONDAY	11 TUESDAY	12 WEDNESDAY
13 THURSDAY	14 FRIDAY	15 SATURDAY
16 SUNDAY	NOTES	

MY WEEK

MARCH

17 MONDAY	18 TUESDAY	19 WEDNESDAY
20 THURSDAY	21 FRIDAY	22 SATURDAY
23 SUNDAY	NOTES	

MY WEEK

MARCH

| 24 MONDAY | 25 TUESDAY | 26 WEDNESDAY |
| 27 THURSDAY | 28 FRIDAY | 29 SATURDAY |

30 SUNDAY

NOTES

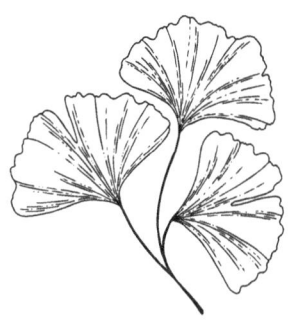

"The most common and the monstrous defect in the education of the day is that children fail to acquire the habit of reading. Knowledge is conveyed to them by lessons and talk, but the studious habit of using books as a means of interest and delight is not so acquired."

Charlotte Mason Page 227 Volume 1

___/___/___   # Quarterly 2 Notes

QUARTERLY PLANNER (DATES)

_____
_____
_____
_____
_____
_____
_____
_____
_____
_____
_____
_____
_____
_____
_____
_____
_____
_____

NOTES

_____
_____
_____
_____
_____
_____
_____
_____
_____
_____
_____
_____
_____
_____
_____
_____
_____
_____

STUDENT HELP AT A GLANCE

MONDAY
TUESDAY
WEDNESDAY
THURSDAY
FRIDAY
SATURDAY
SUNDAY

BOOKS TO GET

_____
_____
_____
_____
_____
_____
_____
_____

PEOPLE TO CONTACT

_____
_____
_____
_____
_____

APRIL

MONDAY	TUESDAY	WEDNESDAY	THURSDAY
31	1	2	3
7	8	9	10
14	15	16	17
21	22	23	24
28	29	30	1

FRIDAY	SATURDAY	SUNDAY
4	5	6
11	12	13
18	19	20
25	26	27
2	3	4

notes

MY WEEK

MARCH - APRIL

| 31 MONDAY | 1 TUESDAY | 2 WEDNESDAY |

| 3 THURSDAY | 4 FRIDAY | 5 SATURDAY |

| 6 SUNDAY | NOTES |

MY WEEK

APRIL

7 MONDAY	8 TUESDAY	9 WEDNESDAY
10 THURSDAY	11 FRIDAY	12 SATURDAY

13 SUNDAY	NOTES

MY WEEK

APRIL

14 MONDAY

15 TUESDAY

16 WEDNESDAY

17 THURSDAY

18 FRIDAY

19 SATURDAY

20 SUNDAY

NOTES

MY WEEK

APRIL

21 MONDAY	22 TUESDAY	23 WEDNESDAY
24 THURSDAY	25 FRIDAY	26 SATURDAY

27 SUNDAY	NOTES

MAY

MONDAY	TUESDAY	WEDNESDAY	THURSDAY
28	29	30	1
5	6	7	8
12	13	14	15
19	20	21	22
26	27	28	29

FRIDAY	SATURDAY	SUNDAY
2	3	4
9	10	11
16	17	18
23	24	25
30	31	1

notes

MY WEEK

APRIL - MAY

28 MONDAY	29 TUESDAY	30 WEDNESDAY
1 THURSDAY	2 FRIDAY	3 SATURDAY
4 SUNDAY	NOTES	

MY WEEK

MAY

5 MONDAY	6 TUESDAY	7 WEDNESDAY
8 THURSDAY	9 FRIDAY	10 SATURDAY
11 SUNDAY	NOTES	

MY WEEK

MAY

12 MONDAY	13 TUESDAY	14 WEDNESDAY
15 THURSDAY	16 FRIDAY	17 SATURDAY
18 SUNDAY	NOTES	

MY WEEK

MAY

19 MONDAY	**20** TUESDAY	**21** WEDNESDAY
22 THURSDAY	**23** FRIDAY	**24** SATURDAY
25 SUNDAY	NOTES	

JUNE

MONDAY	TUESDAY	WEDNESDAY	THURSDAY
26	27	28	29
2	3	4	5
9	10	11	12
16	17	18	19
23	24	25	26
30	1	2	3

FRIDAY	SATURDAY	SUNDAY
30	31	1
6	7	8
13	14	15
20	21	22
27	28	29
4	5	6

notes

MY WEEK

MAY - JUNE

| 26 MONDAY | 27 TUESDAY | 28 WEDNESDAY |

| 29 THURSDAY | 30 FRIDAY | 31 SATURDAY |

| 1 SUNDAY | NOTES |

MY WEEK

JUNE

2 MONDAY	3 TUESDAY	4 WEDNESDAY
5 THURSDAY	6 FRIDAY	7 SATURDAY
8 SUNDAY	NOTES	

MY WEEK

JUNE

9 MONDAY

10 TUESDAY

11 WEDNESDAY

12 THURSDAY

13 FRIDAY

14 SATURDAY

15 SUNDAY

NOTES

MY WEEK

JUNE

16 MONDAY	17 TUESDAY	18 WEDNESDAY
19 THURSDAY	20 FRIDAY	21 SATURDAY
22 SUNDAY	NOTES	

MY WEEK

JUNE

23 MONDAY

24 TUESDAY

25 WEDNESDAY

26 THURSDAY

27 FRIDAY

28 SATURDAY

29 SUNDAY

NOTES

"The child has truly a great deal to do before he is in the condition to 'believe his own eyes'; but Nature teaches so gently, so gradually, so persistently, that he is never overdone, but goes on gathering little stores of knowledge about whatever comes before him."

Charlotte Mason Page 66 Volume 1

Quarterly 3 Notes

QUARTERLY PLANNER (DATES)

_____
_____
_____
_____
_____
_____
_____
_____
_____
_____
_____
_____
_____
_____
_____

NOTES

_____
_____
_____
_____
_____
_____
_____
_____
_____
_____
_____
_____
_____
_____
_____

STUDENT HELP AT A GLANCE

MONDAY
TUESDAY
WEDNESDAY
THURSDAY
FRIDAY
SATURDAY
SUNDAY

BOOKS TO GET

_____
_____
_____
_____
_____
_____
_____

PEOPLE TO CONTACT

_____
_____
_____
_____
_____

JULY

MONDAY	TUESDAY	WEDNESDAY	THURSDAY
30	1	2	3
7	8	9	10
14	15	16	17
21	22	23	24
28	29	30	31

FRIDAY	SATURDAY	SUNDAY
4	5	6
11	12	13
18	19	20
25	26	27
1	2	3

notes

MY WEEK

JUNE - JULY

30 MONDAY	1 TUESDAY	2 WEDNESDAY
3 THURSDAY	4 FRIDAY	5 SATURDAY
6 SUNDAY	NOTES	

MY WEEK

JULY

| 7 MONDAY | 8 TUESDAY | 9 WEDNESDAY |

| 10 THURSDAY | 11 FRIDAY | 12 SATURDAY |

| 13 SUNDAY | NOTES |

MY WEEK

JULY

14 MONDAY

15 TUESDAY

16 WEDNESDAY

17 THURSDAY

18 FRIDAY

19 SATURDAY

20 SUNDAY

NOTES

MY WEEK  JULY

21 MONDAY	22 TUESDAY	23 WEDNESDAY
24 THURSDAY	25 FRIDAY	26 SATURDAY
27 SUNDAY	NOTES	

AUGUST

MONDAY	TUESDAY	WEDNESDAY	THURSDAY
28	29	30	31
4	5	6	7
11	12	13	14
18	19	20	21
25	26	27	28

FRIDAY	SATURDAY	SUNDAY
1	2	3
8	9	10
15	16	17
22	23	24
29	30	31

notes

MY WEEK

JULY - AUGUST

28 MONDAY	29 TUESDAY	30 WEDNESDAY
31 THURSDAY	1 FRIDAY	2 SATURDAY

3 SUNDAY	NOTES

MY WEEK

AUGUST

4 MONDAY	5 TUESDAY	6 WEDNESDAY
7 THURSDAY	8 FRIDAY	9 SATURDAY
10 SUNDAY	NOTES	

MY WEEK

AUGUST

11 MONDAY

12 TUESDAY

13 WEDNESDAY

14 THURSDAY

15 FRIDAY

16 SATURDAY

17 SUNDAY

NOTES

MY WEEK

AUGUST

18 MONDAY	19 TUESDAY	20 WEDNESDAY
21 THURSDAY	22 FRIDAY	23 SATURDAY
24 SUNDAY	NOTES	

MY WEEK

AUGUST

| 25 MONDAY | 26 TUESDAY | 27 WEDNESDAY |
| 28 THURSDAY | 29 FRIDAY | 30 SATURDAY |

31 SUNDAY

NOTES

"The teacher who allows his scholars the freedom of the city of books is at liberty to be their guide, philosopher and friend; and no longer the mere instrument of forcible intellectual feeding."

Charlotte Mason Page 32 Volume 6

SEPTEMBER

MONDAY	TUESDAY	WEDNESDAY	THURSDAY
1	2	3	4
8	9	10	11
15	16	17	18
22	23	24	25
29	30	1	2

FRIDAY	SATURDAY	SUNDAY
5	6	7
12	13	14
19	20	21
26	27	28
3	4	5

notes

MY WEEK

SEPTEMBER

1 MONDAY	2 TUESDAY	3 WEDNESDAY
4 THURSDAY	5 FRIDAY	6 SATURDAY
7 SUNDAY	NOTES	

MY WEEK

SEPTEMBER

8 MONDAY	9 TUESDAY	10 WEDNESDAY
11 THURSDAY	12 FRIDAY	13 SATURDAY

14 SUNDAY	NOTES

MY WEEK

SEPTEMBER

15 MONDAY

16 TUESDAY

17 WEDNESDAY

18 THURSDAY

19 FRIDAY

20 SATURDAY

21 SUNDAY

NOTES

MY WEEK

SEPTEMBER

22 MONDAY	23 TUESDAY	24 WEDNESDAY
25 THURSDAY	26 FRIDAY	27 SATURDAY

28 SUNDAY	NOTES

Quarterly 4 Notes

QUARTERLY PLANNER (DATES)

_____
_____
_____
_____
_____
_____
_____
_____
_____
_____
_____
_____
_____
_____
_____
_____

NOTES

_____
_____
_____
_____
_____
_____
_____
_____
_____
_____
_____
_____
_____
_____
_____
_____

STUDENT HELP AT A GLANCE

MONDAY
TUESDAY
WEDNESDAY
THURSDAY
FRIDAY
SATURDAY
SUNDAY

BOOKS TO GET

_____
_____
_____
_____
_____
_____
_____

PEOPLE TO CONTACT

_____
_____
_____
_____
_____

OCTOBER

MONDAY	TUESDAY	WEDNESDAY	THURSDAY
29	30	1	2
6	7	8	9
13	14	15	16
20	21	22	23
27	28	29	30

FRIDAY	SATURDAY	SUNDAY
3	4	5
10	11	12
17	18	19
24	25	26
31	1	2

notes

MY WEEK

SEPTEMBER - OCTOBER

29 MONDAY	30 TUESDAY	1 WEDNESDAY
2 THURSDAY	3 FRIDAY	4 SATURDAY
5 SUNDAY	NOTES	

MY WEEK

OCTOBER

| 6 MONDAY | 7 TUESDAY | 8 WEDNESDAY |
| 9 THURSDAY | 10 FRIDAY | 11 SATURDAY |

| 12 SUNDAY | NOTES |

MY WEEK

OCTOBER

| 13 MONDAY | 14 TUESDAY | 15 WEDNESDAY |
| 16 THURSDAY | 17 FRIDAY | 18 SATURDAY |

| 19 SUNDAY | NOTES |

MY WEEK  OCTOBER

20 MONDAY	21 TUESDAY	22 WEDNESDAY
23 THURSDAY	24 FRIDAY	25 SATURDAY
26 SUNDAY	NOTES	

NOVEMBER

MONDAY	TUESDAY	WEDNESDAY	THURSDAY
27	28	29	30
3	4	5	6
10	11	12	13
17	18	19	20
24	25	26	27

FRIDAY	SATURDAY	SUNDAY	notes
31	1	2	
7	8	9	
14	15	16	
21	22	23	
28	29	30	

MY WEEK

OCTOBER - NOVEMBER

27 MONDAY	28 TUESDAY	29 WEDNESDAY
30 THURSDAY	31 FRIDAY	1 SATURDAY

2 SUNDAY	NOTES

MY WEEK

NOVEMBER

3 MONDAY	4 TUESDAY	5 WEDNESDAY
6 THURSDAY	7 FRIDAY	8 SATURDAY
9 SUNDAY	NOTES	

MY WEEK

NOVEMBER

10 MONDAY

11 TUESDAY

12 WEDNESDAY

13 THURSDAY

14 FRIDAY

15 SATURDAY

16 SUNDAY

NOTES

MY WEEK

NOVEMBER

17 MONDAY	18 TUESDAY	19 WEDNESDAY
20 THURSDAY	21 FRIDAY	22 SATURDAY

23 SUNDAY	NOTES

MY WEEK  NOVEMBER

24 MONDAY	25 TUESDAY	26 WEDNESDAY
27 THURSDAY	28 FRIDAY	29 SATURDAY
30 SUNDAY	NOTES	

"Our business is to give children the great ideas of life, of religion, history and science; but it is the ideas we must give, clothed upon the facts as they occur, and we must leave the child to deal with these as he chooses."

Charlotte Mason

DECEMBER

MONDAY	TUESDAY	WEDNESDAY	THURSDAY
1	2	3	4
8	9	10	11
15	16	17	18
22	23	24	25
29	30	31	1

FRIDAY	SATURDAY	SUNDAY
5	6	7
12	13	14
19	20	21
26	27	28
2	3	4

notes

MY WEEK

DECEMBER

1 MONDAY	2 TUESDAY	3 WEDNESDAY
4 THURSDAY	5 FRIDAY	6 SATURDAY
7 SUNDAY	NOTES	

MY WEEK

DECEMBER

8 MONDAY	9 TUESDAY	10 WEDNESDAY
11 THURSDAY	12 FRIDAY	13 SATURDAY

14 SUNDAY	NOTES

MY WEEK

DECEMBER

15 MONDAY	16 TUESDAY	17 WEDNESDAY
18 THURSDAY	19 FRIDAY	20 SATURDAY
21 SUNDAY	NOTES	

MY WEEK

DECEMBER

22 MONDAY	23 TUESDAY	24 WEDNESDAY
25 THURSDAY	26 FRIDAY	27 SATURDAY

28 SUNDAY	NOTES

MY WEEK

DECEMBER

29 MONDAY	30 TUESDAY	31 WEDNESDAY
1 THURSDAY	2 FRIDAY	3 SATURDAY

4 SUNDAY	NOTES

2026

Quarterly 1 Notes

__/__/__

QUARTERLY PLANNER (DATES)

_____
_____
_____
_____
_____
_____
_____
_____
_____
_____
_____
_____
_____
_____
_____
_____
_____

NOTES

_____
_____
_____
_____
_____
_____
_____
_____
_____
_____
_____
_____
_____
_____
_____
_____
_____

STUDENT HELP AT A GLANCE

MONDAY
TUESDAY
WEDNESDAY
THURSDAY
FRIDAY
SATURDAY
SUNDAY

BOOKS TO GET

_____
_____
_____
_____
_____
_____
_____
_____

PEOPLE TO CONTACT

_____
_____
_____
_____
_____
_____

JANUARY

MONDAY	TUESDAY	WEDNESDAY	THURSDAY
29	30	31	1
5	6	7	8
12	13	14	15
19	20	21	22
26	27	28	29

FRIDAY	SATURDAY	SUNDAY
2	3	4
9	10	11
16	17	18
23	24	25
30	31	1

notes

MY WEEK

JANUARY

5 MONDAY

6 TUESDAY

7 WEDNESDAY

8 THURSDAY

9 FRIDAY

10 SATURDAY

11 SUNDAY

NOTES

MY WEEK

JANUARY

12 MONDAY	13 TUESDAY	14 WEDNESDAY
15 THURSDAY	16 FRIDAY	17 SATURDAY
18 SUNDAY	NOTES	

MY WEEK

JANUARY

19 MONDAY	20 TUESDAY	21 WEDNESDAY
22 THURSDAY	23 FRIDAY	24 SATURDAY
25 SUNDAY	NOTES	

"Educating the mind without educating the heart is no education at all."

Aristotle

FEBRUARY

MONDAY	TUESDAY	WEDNESDAY	THURSDAY
26	27	28	29
2	3	4	5
9	10	11	12
16	17	18	19
23	24	25	26

FRIDAY	SATURDAY	SUNDAY
30	31	1
6	7	8
13	14	15
20	21	22
27	28	1

notes

MY WEEK

JANUARY

| 26 MONDAY | 27 TUESDAY | 28 WEDNESDAY |
| 29 THURSDAY | 30 FRIDAY | 31 SATURDAY |

1 SUNDAY

NOTES

MY WEEK

FEBRUARY

2 MONDAY	3 TUESDAY	4 WEDNESDAY
5 THURSDAY	6 FRIDAY	7 SATURDAY
8 SUNDAY	NOTES	

MY WEEK

FEBRUARY

| 9 MONDAY | 10 TUESDAY | 11 WEDNESDAY |
| 12 THURSDAY | 13 FRIDAY | 14 SATURDAY |

15 SUNDAY

NOTES

MY WEEK

FEBRUARY

16 MONDAY	17 TUESDAY	18 WEDNESDAY
19 THURSDAY	20 FRIDAY	21 SATURDAY
22 SUNDAY	NOTES	

MARCH

MONDAY	TUESDAY	WEDNESDAY	THURSDAY
23	24	25	26
2	3	4	5
9	10	11	12
16	17	18	19
23	24	25	26
30	31	1	2

FRIDAY	SATURDAY	SUNDAY
27	28	1
6	7	8
13	14	15
20	21	22
27	28	29
3	4	5

notes

MY WEEK

FEBRUARY - MARCH

23 MONDAY	24 TUESDAY	25 WEDNESDAY
26 THURSDAY	27 FRIDAY	28 SATURDAY
1 SUNDAY	NOTES	

MY WEEK

MARCH

2 MONDAY	3 TUESDAY	4 WEDNESDAY
5 THURSDAY	6 FRIDAY	7 SATURDAY
8 SUNDAY	NOTES	

MY WEEK

MARCH

| 9 MONDAY | 10 TUESDAY | 11 WEDNESDAY |

| 12 THURSDAY | 13 FRIDAY | 14 SATURDAY |

| 15 SUNDAY | NOTES |

MY WEEK

MARCH

16 MONDAY

17 TUESDAY

18 WEDNESDAY

19 THURSDAY

20 FRIDAY

21 SATURDAY

22 SUNDAY

NOTES

MY WEEK

MARCH

23 MONDAY

24 TUESDAY

25 WEDNESDAY

26 THURSDAY

27 FRIDAY

28 SATURDAY

29 SUNDAY

NOTES

MY WEEK

MARCH - APRIL

30 MONDAY	31 TUESDAY	1 WEDNESDAY
2 THURSDAY	3 FRIDAY	4 SATURDAY
5 SUNDAY	NOTES	

LISTS & RECORDS

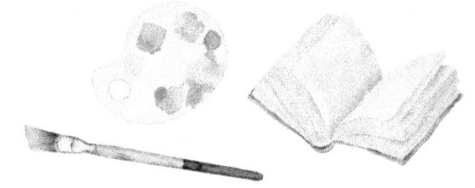

Art Appreciation

ARTWORK & ARTIST   **DATE**

Artwork & Artist	Date

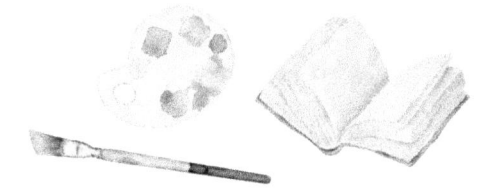

Art Appreciation

ARTWORK & ARTIST **DATE**

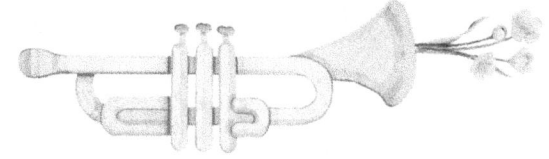

Music Appreciation

MUSIC & COMPOSER | **DATE**

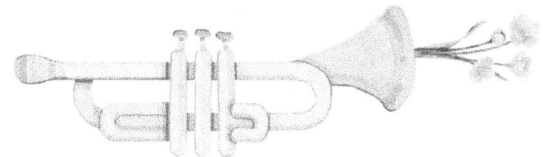

Music Appreciation

MUSIC & COMPOSER   **DATE**

Poetry List

POEMS & POETS	DATE

Poetry List

POEMS & POETS **DATE**

Movies & Documentaries

MOVIES & DOCUMENTARIES	DATE

Movies & Documentaries

MOVIES & DOCUMENTARIES	DATE

Field Trips & Nature Walks

TRIPS & WALKS   **DATE**

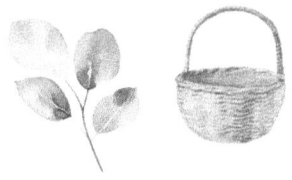

Field Trips & Nature Walks

TRIPS & WALKS   **DATE**

Book List

TITLE & AUTHOR   **DATE**

Book List

TITLE & AUTHOR | **DATE**

Book List

TITLE & AUTHOR   **DATE**

Book List

TITLE & AUTHOR **DATE**

Books on Loan to Friends

TITLE & AUTHOR	NAME OF BORROWER	DATE LENT	RETURNED

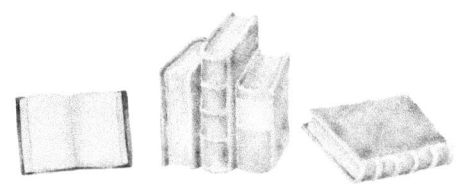

Books on Loan to Friends

TITLE & AUTHOR	NAME OF BORROWER	DATE LENT	RETURNED

Homeschool Expenses

PURCHASES	DATE	COST	NOTES

Homeschool Expenses

PURCHASES	DATE	COST	NOTES

Wish List

ITEM	COST	NOTES

Wish List

ITEM	COST	NOTES

_____ List

_____ List

Projects & Ideas

Projects & Ideas

Student Notes

NAME _____

Student Notes

NAME _____

Student Notes

NAME _____

Student Notes

NAME _____

Student Notes

NAME _____

Student Notes

NAME _____

Notes

Notes

Notes

Notes

Notes

www.ingramcontent.com/pod-product-compliance
Lightning Source LLC
Chambersburg PA
CBHW082246090526
44585CB00021BA/2459

9781763629127